Evolving English
EXPLORED

Julian Walker

D1335072

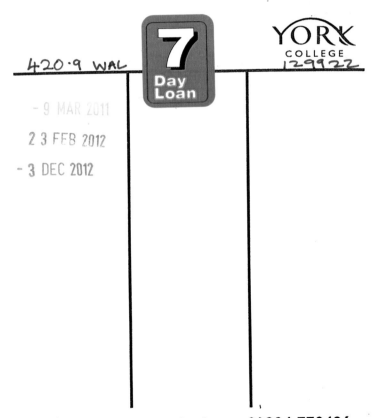

**To renew please telephone: 01904 770406
with your ID card number**

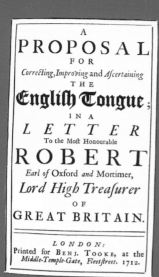

A
PROPOSAL
FOR
Correcting, Improving and *Ascertaining*
THE
English Tongue;
IN A
LETTER
To the Most Honourable
ROBERT
Earl of Oxford *and* Mortimer,
Lord High Treasurer
OF
GREAT BRITAIN.

LONDON:
Printed for BENJ. TOOKE, at the
Middle-Temple-Gate, Fleetstreet. 1712.

The year was 1712. English was in a mess. New words were being invented or adopted every day, slang words were poisoning the language, spelling was variable and, worst of all, the French had an academy to maintain the purity of their language. Should not English have one too, asked one of the great writers of the day, an institution that would suppress 'corruptions' and the 'spoiling of the English tongue'?

Fast forward to the twenty-first century: a BBC journalist wishes the basic rules of grammar were still taught to every child, 'inflammable' means the same as 'flammable', a writer proposes a 'zero tolerance approach to punctuation', and the Queen's English Society (with the intention of keeping English 'safe from declining standards') has a website called 'The QES English Academy' which it claims 'no-one can afford to ignore and which everyone needs to draw upon'.

So, how did we get to this permanent state of change punctuated by outbursts of panic? How has this mongrel language, with its devouring of foreign words, its grammar that nobody seems to learn, its contradictory spelling and social class divisions, provided the world with some of its greatest literature and come to be currently the world's most widely used language?

We can say that there is no one simple 'story' of English; that much is clear from the difference between spoken and written English. As a result of its dissemination around the world, English does not 'belong' to England, in the sense of there being a 'pure standard'; nor has there been an individual or a group of persons with any right to prescribe what a standard should be. It is adapted by all its users, and always has been, and without users it is a shadow of a language. As a continuously changing language it provides a rich ground for study in innumerable ways.

conventional, than strictly accurate. **The Queen (God bless her!) is of course no more the proprietor of the English language than any one of us.** Nor does she, nor do the

For more than 500 years, the structure, spelling, usages, grammar and history of the English language have fascinated speakers and scholars, leading to detailed study of local variation, reconstruction of historical pronunciation, and close analysis of word-use by specific authors. Henry Alford, who wrote on current English in 1864, was able to show that an eighteenth-century pastiche on medieval writing was fake purely on the grounds of its repeated use of the word 'its', which occurred only three times in Shakespeare, and only once in *Paradise Lost* (1667).

But the study of English is not without pitfalls.

English has been burdened by several stories which may be generously called apocryphal. For example, the story that there is an area in the US where the speech-forms of Shakespeare's time have been retained; or the idea that 'posh' was formed from the phrase 'port out, starboard home' for the more expensive shaded cabins on liners going between Britain and India; or the idea that people spoke English better 50 years ago than they do today.

What can be said with certainty is that the language is changing now; there are many reasons for it to go on changing, and in doing so it may break up into several languages. For the history of the English language is a history of change.

JAM of *Cherries, Raspberries,* &c. [prob. of *J' aime,* i. e. I *love it*; as Children used to say in *French* formerly, when they liked any Thing] a Sweetmeat.

Oi! Writing and Speaking

While most English speakers read Standard English every day, few speak it; there are fundamental differences between written and spoken English.

As a spoken statement, 'We need volunteers to help stroke victims', with the stress on the word 'stroke', carries little risk of ambiguity; as a written statement it can be interpreted in two ways, with neither being the obvious – though an intentional pun would be unlikely here.

Complex planning of what you are going to say, ahead of saying it, rarely happens in conversation, while the evidence of writers' drafts and the potential for easy corrections in digital writing systems show that we constantly correct our writing. In speech we rely on social context, intonation, pauses and volume to convey information, none of which are provided in written texts. But written texts can convey their own contextual information, depending on whether they are handwritten or printed, on billboards or pamphlets or the back of an envelope. A number of writers have expressed the need for a font that would be called 'Ironics', to make the writer's intention clear.

Transcribed speech shows it to be full of phrases like 'you know' and 'um, er', thinking space-fillers which are just omitted in written texts. In the playwright Harold Pinter's work *Apart From That* (2006), based on a mobile phone conversation, which very closely approximates directly transcribed speech, it is interesting to note that it is only when we read it aloud that we see that 'you know' is not functioning as a space-filler, but to mean 'I think you know what I mean'.

There are also forms that are neither exclusively spoken or written English. Text messaging formulated within a medium of speech (the phone) is clearly conducive to usages from shorthand and rebuses, where pictures take the place of words – C U 2nite, for example, uses phonetic symbols which make sense when read aloud. But it is noteworthy that some people feel that the spelling 'thanx' or 'thx', a product of limited-character SMS phone messages, is pointless, and even disrespectful.

As swearing is so much associated with the spoken language, it has posed problems for writers, especially writers of texts for performance. The first performance of George Bernard Shaw's *Pygmalion* was preceded in 1913 by much excited anticipation of the use of the word 'bloody'; would it be censored or banned? In the event the Lord Chamberlain's office allowed the text, though some linguists reckoned Eliza would have said 'no bleedin' fear' rather than 'no bloody fear'.

In Tony Harrison's poem *V* (1985) there are conversations between the poet writing and a person speaking in dialect, with words spelt to reflect both dialect and accent.

'OK, forget the aspirations. Look, I know
United's losing gets you fans incensed
and how far the HARP inside you makes you go
but *all* these Vs: against! against! against!'

*Ah'll tell yer then what really riles a bloke.
It's reading on their graves the jobs they did –
butcher, publican and baker. Me, I'll croak
doing t'same nowt ah do now as a kid.*

How often do we use the phrase 'you know'?

A quick look at TV and radio interviews with Britain's last three Prime Ministers shows them saying 'you know' on average once every 20 seconds.

Making your Mark

The first writing in Old English was in runes, a writing system used throughout northern Europe. Runes arrived in East Anglia from Scandinavia some years before the first documented Anglo-Saxon invasion in the fifth century.

ᚱ ᚠ ᛋ ᚻ ᚠ ᛏ
ᚢ ᛗ ᛗ ᚻ ᛫ ᚠ ᚷ ᛏ ᛗ ᛫ ᚷ ᚷ ᚷ

Their use continued until the eighth century, though missionaries introduced the Roman alphabet in the late sixth century.

The earliest role of punctuation was to indicate to the reader – reading aloud – how to read the text: primarily where to stop while reading and how long for. This has changed, particularly in the past 400 years. The role of indicating breaks remains, but now punctuation, including the use of paragraphs and italics, mainly directs or changes the sense of what is being read. Inconsistencies and uncertain usages remain: the famous grocer's apostrophe; well known, well-known, or wellknown; and The Nobel Prize in Medicine or the Nobel prize in medicine?

The changing nature of mark-making can be seen in the fact that we now tend to write by hand less than we send text messages, use a keyboard, or press number-code buttons. Yet many of us need to go back no more than a few generations to find ancestors who made their mark on documents with a cross. Will handwriting turn out to have been just a temporary skill?

ৎ৶   ৎ৶   ৎ৶   ৎ৶   ৎ৶   ৎ৶   ৎ৶

The ivy leaf, used in Old English manuscripts to indicate a major break within a text, survived as a printers' decorative device.

POTATOE'S
50p /lb

The Norman takeover of England in 1066 led to less writing in English and more in Latin and Anglo-Norman French, with the consequent gradual disappearance of certain Old English letter forms – ash, thorn, eth, wynn and yogh.

œ þ ð ƿ ȝ

YE OLDE MISREADING

Thorn, pronounced 'th', became a similar shape to 'y' during the Middle English period (c.1100–1300 to 1550), and later readers mistook it for a 'y' sound, hence the mistaken archaisms such as 'ye olde tea shoppe'.

The early English printer William Caxton used the slash, the stop and the colon to indicate speech patterns for the reciter of a text, but they bear no relation to how these symbols are used today.

Margarete by the grace of god . Du- jopne of Lotryk of Brabande zc /

The introduction of typography led to some long-lasting inconsistencies: 'u' and 'v' were more or less interchangeable during the sixteenth century, and the distinction between 'i' and 'j' was not established until the mid-seventeenth century. Until the late eighteenth century compositors, who made up the text, used a 'long s' (looking very much like 'f' except that the bar was only on the left of the upright) at the beginning or in the middle of words; but the 'long s' persisted in handwriting into the 1850s.

The apostrophe was introduced in the sixteenth century, but it was not until the late nineteenth century that printers and writers tried to set out rules as to how to use it, many of which were apparently arbitrary. For example: John's leg, the dog's leg, its leg. Why no apostrophe in 'its'?

Change – Saxon to Caxton

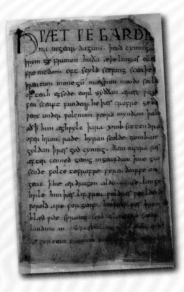

According to Bede, a monk writing in the early eighth century, the Anglo-Saxons arrived in the mid-fifth century, driving westwards the Celtic-speaking Britons, some of whom ended up being called Welsh – meaning 'foreigners'. The incomers brought with them Germanic dialects which developed into various dialects of what we now call Old English, a language used for epic poetry, lawgiving, religion, education and everyday conversation. This was the language of major works such as *Beowulf* and the *Anglo-Saxon Chronicle*. Old English absorbed words and structures from Latin and later Old Norse, but suffered a major reversal of fortune at Hastings in October 1066.

There is a well-known story that after the Conquest, England was characterised by the Saxon peasant in the field, who could only tend the animals, which he knew by the Old English words 'cows', 'sheep' and 'pigs'; and his Norman overlord, sitting at his table, who knew them as 'beef', 'mutton' and 'pork', all French words. The reality is that after the dispossession of the Saxon nobility, the Norman lords needed to communicate with their new vassals, and ambitious English-speakers would have learned the speech of their new masters. A hundred years after the Conquest Richard FitzNeal wrote that 'one can hardly tell today who is of English and who of Norman race'.

In England after 1066 Latin, the language of the church, replaced Old English as the language of administration, while Anglo-Norman French became the language of power. The influence of Latin and French on English can be seen in the large number of words adopted. Often a French or Latin word, or sometimes both, would be adopted even though there was already an Old English equivalent which continued to be used.

"You mean this comes from an animal?"

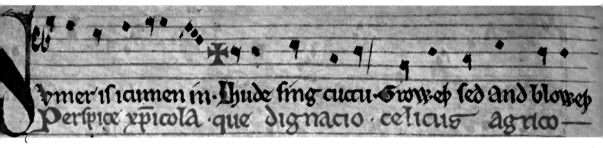

There are few records in English from the post-Conquest period – there was no court patronage for literature in English. From what we do have we know that both before and after the Conquest Old English evolved, as the meaning of a sentence came to be expressed more by the order of words than different grammatical endings to words.

In the *Kentish Homilies*, a book of prayers of the twelfth century, we find the meaning of the words modified by different endings, and there are still Old English symbols, but the word order is very close to Modern English.

The period of transition from Old English to the emergence of Middle English is usually given as 1100 to 1300 – quite a lot of the song *Sumer is icumen in* from the mid-thirteenth century is fairly straightforward to read.

English has a very rich vocabulary, and often there are a number of words that express one idea. One reason for this is that we have a word from Old English (ask) and one from French (demand) and often one from Latin too (interrogate). But is there a status difference between them?

Sound

TO A.

L O U S E,

On Seeing one on a Lady's Bonnet at Church.

HA! whare ye gaun, ye crowlan ferlie!
  Your impudence protects you fairly:
I canna fay but ye ftrunt rarely,
      Owre *gawze* and *lace*;
Tho' faith, I fear ye dine but fparely,
      On fic a place.

Ye ugly, creepan, blaftet wonner,
Detefted, fhunn'd, by faunt an' finner;

I'd gie you fic a hearty dofe o't,
      Wad drefs your droddum!

I wad na been furpriz'd to fpy
You on an auld wife's *flainen toy*;
Or aiblins fome bit duddie boy,
      On's *wylecoat*;
But Mifs's fine *Lunardi*, fye!
      How daur ye do't?

O *Jenny* dinna tofs your head,
An' fet your beauties a' abread!
Ye little ken what curfed fpeed
      The blaftie's makin!
Thae *winks* and *finger-ends*, I dread,
      Are notice takin!

O wad fome Pow'r the giftie gie us
To fee ourfels as others fee us!
It wad frae monie a blunder free us
      An' foolifh notion:
What airs in drefs an' gait wad lea'e us,
      And ev'n Devotion!

How do we know what speech sounded like before sound-recording was available? A number of ways: spelling, poetry and, from the seventeenth century onwards, people writing about speech.

Though English spelling frequently looks absurd it does give a clear indication of how a word was pronounced when it first entered the language. Consider the word 'knight' – it developed from the word *cniht*, originally meaning 'boy', which entered English before AD 700. It was almost certainly spoken with all the letters pronounced, as it is in the modern Dutch word *knecht*.

Poetry helps, for example the following lines from Pope's *The Rape of the Lock*:
Here thou, great Anna!
Whom three realms obey,
Dost sometimes counsel take
– and sometimes tea.

This supports the idea that in London in 1714 'tea' rhymed with 'obey'; of course countless other comparisons are required to confirm this. Rhythm and alliteration also help us to deduce pronunciation, as does dialect spelling as used by writers such as Robert Burns or D H Lawrence.

Ben Jonson's *English Grammar* of 1640 was one of a number of books of the period which looked at how people spoke, and gave clear physiological descriptions of speech, for example showing how the word 'rarer' was pronounced.

R

(*x*) Is the *Dogs* Letter, and hurreth in the found; the tongue ftriking the inner palate, with a trembling about the teeth. It is founded firme in the beginning of the words, and more *liquid* in the middle, and ends: as in

rarer. riper.

> **THOROUGH,** *thur'ro.* prepos. (318).
> By way of making paffage or penetration;
> by means of, commonly written, Through;
> which fee.
> **THOROUGH,** *thûr'rô.* a. (390).
> Complete, full, perfect; paffing through.

Commentaries and changes in spellings and rhymes
show us that the way people pronounced vowels changed
between about 1400 and 1600, with some important
later changes. For example, Chaucer in the late fourteenth
century would have pronounced 'down' as 'doon',
while Shakespeare 200 years later pronounced it more
like 'deuwn'; but Shakespeare pronounced 'clean' as
'clane', a pronunciation which changed over the
following century.

During the eighteenth century, the rise of a wealthy
bourgeoisie hoping to 'enter society' allowed Thomas
Sheridan, the writer of *Lectures on Elocution* (1762) to
make a fortune, as people attempted to acquire the 'just
and graceful management of the voice, countenance and
gesture, in speaking'. John Walker's *Pronouncing Dictionary*
(1791) provided people with an authority for pronunciation,
which allows us 200 years later to recreate a standard
pronunciation for late-eighteenth-century word-sounds,
e.g. 'thorough', pronounced to rhyme with 'burrow'.

There is a crackly recording of Florence Nightingale
speaking in 1890, which is fairly easy to understand;
her vowel sounds contrast with those of Eliza Doolittle i
n *Pygmalion*, which Shaw transcribes as 'Ah-ah-ah-ow-ow-
oo-oo!!!', and Higgins describes as 'such depressing and
disgusting sounds'.

The vowel sound most frequently used in Received Pronunciation is the first sound
in the word 'about'. No surprises there. But you might be surprised to learn that 'n'
is the consonant sound most frequently used.

Accent and Dialect – The British Isles

Very few people speak Standard English with Received Pronunciation (around 2% of the UK population); some of us speak in dialect (local words, grammar and pronunciation), and most of us speak with a local accent (how we sound).

In *Beowulf* there are a number of identifiable regional dialects – early and late West Saxon, East Anglian, Mercian, Northumbrian, Kentish – and a range of dialects can be seen in the Middle English period as local stories and tales were written down. Chaucer's *Reeve's Tale*, in the late fourteenth century, is the first known story in English to make use of distinctly different and identifiable dialects, in this case for comic effect.

Standard English: conventional vocabulary and generally approved grammatical forms; widely promoted in educational contexts.

Received Pronunciation: regionally neutral, middle-class English accent associated with the BBC; widely used as a model for teaching English as a foreign language.

Attitudes to regional accents have varied over time – Thomas Sheridan's choice of words clearly indicated his view in 1762 – 'those who endeavour to cure themselves of a provincial or vicious pronunciation'. From the end of the eighteenth century writers such as Robert Burns, Maria Edgeworth, Emily Brontë, Charles Dickens and Thomas Hardy used accent as a way of delineating character and place, making readers aware of variety in speech within the medium of respectable literature. Nineteenth-century dialect poetry such as the *Yorkshire Garland* or works by William Barnes in Dorset, helped spread the appreciation of dialect as a literary form of English.

John Ray's *Collection of English Words* (1674) marks dialect as a new area of study. By 1900 Joseph Wright, in his *Dialect Dictionary*, was concerned that dialects were already vanishing fast. The continued awareness of this has given urgency to the collecting of dialects in the Survey of English Dialects, the *Dictionary of American Regional English*, and BBC Voices, while the British Library and the University of Leeds continue to record and analyse regional voices.

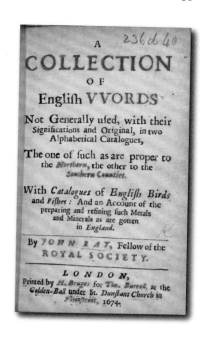

Children pick up their local accent by the age of three, and when a family moves to a different area the children are the first to pick up the new accent. But the family is also a forum for the continuation of an accent. Following the establishment of the New Towns after the Second World War, a cockney accent is as likely to be heard in Milton Keynes or Basildon as Lewisham or Stratford, where a multi-ethnic population is creating its own accent, drawn from a range of places including Bangladesh, Jamaica and Nigeria. 'Jafaican', typified by Ali G, may be seen as a disparaging term, but if so it echoes 'cockney', which in Chaucer's day meant 'an effeminate townsman'.

FLU. To the mines! tell you the duke, it is not so good to come to the mines; for, look you, the mines is not according to the disciplines of the war: the concavities of it is not sufficient; for, look you, th' athversary, you may discuss unto the duke, look you, is digt himself four yard under the countermines: by Cheshu, I think a' will plow up all, if there is not better directions.

Several nineteenth and twentieth century writers, such as H G Wells, Rudyard Kipling and D H Lawrence, as well as recent writers like Roddy Doyle and Irvine Welsh, adapt spelling to show clearly the accent of a speaker. Even Shakespeare used this in Fluellen's speech in *Henry V.* Does this inform or obstruct the reading of the text?

Change –
The Last 500 Years

During the sixteenth century the status of English was raised through the Church's need, following the Reformation, to provide authorised translations of the Bible (following on from the first translations in the fourteenth century) and the creation of the *Book of Common Prayer*. The first vernacular dictionaries placed English on a par with Latin and Greek. Scholars such as Hart and Mulcaster began to study and organise the language, writing grammars, spelling guides and, in the early seventeenth century, the first English dictionaries. The Authorised Version of the Bible (1611), which was quickly disseminated around the country, established a prestigious, if consciously conservative, form of the text which had a lasting influence on the language.

There are a number of differences to be found between the middle and the end of the eighteenth century: Lowth's 1762 *Grammar* gives 'holpen' rather than 'helped', 'gotten' rather than 'got', and 'hoven' rather than 'heaved'. Johnson's 1755 *Dictionary* gave 'civick' and 'citess' (a townswoman), and shows 'take' being used to mean 'receive with fondness', where we would now use 'take to', which he does not list.

The flourishing of intellectual life in a number of new fields brought with it a sudden growth in vocabulary, while the rise of literacy, pamphleteering and popular journalism meant that reading was no longer the province of the rich few; in 1667 Samuel Pepys noted a shepherd's boy reading the Bible. Greater diversity, which in the minds of writers such as John Dryden and Jonathan Swift meant the danger of chaos, could only be controlled by some official linguistic authority.

The rules, such as they were, were formulated by works such as Samuel Johnson's mighty 1755 *Dictionary*, with illustrations drawn from 'the best writers' – Johnson's selection of course. The practices proposed in Lowth's *Grammar*, Sheridan's *Lectures on Elocution* (both 1762) and Walker's *Pronouncing Dictionary* (1791) were interpreted by generations of teachers as the rules for 'correct English'.

CI'VICK. *adj.* [*civicus*, Latin.] Relating to civil honours or practises; not military.
        With equal rays immortal Tully shone :
    Behind, Rome's genius waits with *civick* crowns,
    And the great father of his country owns. *Pop. Tem. of Fame.*

bling, *n.* and *adj.*

slang (orig. in the language of rap and hip-hop).

A. *n.* (A piece of) ostentatious jewellery. Hence: wealth; conspicuous consumption.

B. *adj.* Ostentatious, flashy; designating flamboyant jewellery or dress. Also: that glorifies conspicuous consumption; materialistic.

Work on what was to become the *Oxford English Dictionary* began in 1857, providing a continuing study of – and reference for – the language. Starting from a premise of describing rather than prescribing, the *OED*'s aim to be 'the definitive guide to the English language' has brought it enormous influence. Its former reliance on documentation from sources of a certain status restricted its observations to Standard English, and while the range of its sources has widened, the *OED* is still primarily about the written language.

In the twentieth century most changes in Standard English were superficial. But colloquial usage changed often and fast: in football, goals used to be 'taken' not 'scored', 'I am going on well' was an acceptable statement on a First World War field-service postcard, and 'set up' lost its former usage as meaning 'conceited'. The number of words in English multiplied vastly, as improved communications, finance, technological production and travel provided rapidly expanding markets with the need for new words and terminology.

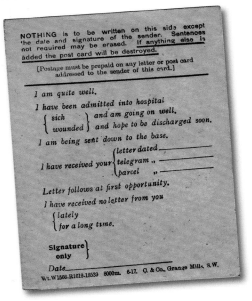

NOTHING is to be written on this side except the date and signature of the sender. Sentences not required may be erased. If anything else is added the post card will be destroyed.

[Postage must be prepaid on any letter or post card addressed to the sender of this card.]

I am quite well.

I have been admitted into hospital
{ sick } and am going on well.
{ wounded } and hope to be discharged soon.

I am being sent down to the base.

I have received your { letter dated _____
{ telegram ,, _____
{ parcel ,, _____

Letter follows at first opportunity.

I have received no letter from you
{ lately
{ for a long time.

Signature }
only }

Date_____
Wt.W1566-R1619-18539 8000m. 8-17. O. & Co., Grange Mills, S.W.

A dish called 'cream ice' was served in 1671; by 1688 it was called 'iced cream', and 'ice cream' from 1744. From about 1880 people began to write it alternatively as 'ice-cream'.

English at Work

In *The Doctor's Dilemma* (1906) George Bernard Shaw wrote that 'all professions are conspiracies against the laity'. Certainly the language of some professions conspires to keep the uninitiated in the dark, sometimes unintentionally, sometimes not.

From the point where English was able to define separate professions, work-specific jargon appeared. Old English leechbooks (books of medicinal recipes) show an early use of terms specific to that profession, no doubt used to boost status and authority.

Accounts from Ely Abbey from the early eleventh century show English being used for the everyday running of such an institution, and a few legal documents written in English during the Norman period have survived. In the Middle English period we see the manipulation of work-specific language to the advantage of the professional, particularly in the field of finance. In 1360 'purveyors' responsible for purchasing on behalf of the Crown realised that their reputation for corruption was such that their jobs needed rebranding. They became 'achatours' (from the French *acheter*, meaning 'to buy'); unfortunately awareness of their dishonesty continued, and their name, which developed into 'escheators', gave us the modern word 'cheat'. In the Prologue to the *Canterbury Tales* Chaucer's Merchant's bad debts and illegal dealings are disguised with the financial jargon-word 'chevyssaunce', which later came to mean the processes of evading laws against lending for profit.

Late-medieval cookery books expected their readers to know not just terms of kitchen preparation but also some anatomy. The *Boke of Kokery* of about 1450 required the cook to 'skoche' (cut) a pike in two or three pieces in the back, to slit the 'pouch' (stomach) and keep the 'fey' (liver). The *Boke of Keruyinge*, 1519, taught the words for carving each kind of animal, including 'dysfygure that pecocke, untache that curlewe, alaye that fesande'.

¶ Heron rosted

¶ Take a heron. lete him blode as a crane. And sue him in al poyntes as a crane. in stalding. dralbing and kuttyng the bone of the nekke a vey And lete the skyn be on &c. roste him and sause him as þe crane. take alwey the bone fro the bac to þe fote. And lete the skyn &c.

Robert Hooke's *Micrographia* (1665), published by the
Royal Society, dates from a period of growing scientific
empiricism, in which experimentation was favoured
above textual authority. Hooke is describing scientific
observations made with microscope and telescope, many
of them for the first time. Though he uses new words such as
'crustaceous' and 'peristaltic', his style of writing is almost
conversational as he describes the process of looking.

During the nineteenth and twentieth centuries the
increasingly specialist nature of science required specialist
language, taking it beyond the comprehension of non-
specialists; science journalism acted as a mediator between
the expert and the layperson.

Work jargon often uses common words for specific
metaphorical applications: in Hooson's *Miners Dictionary*
(1747) a 'horse' was a block of wood on a rope that a miner
sat on to ascend or descend a mine-shaft. A hundred years
later ascending railtrucks in mines or quarries were fitted
with a 'cow', a pronged brake which worked by gravity.

The communication of policy within an organisation
has been a fertile ground for the production of
gobbledegook for decades. Since 1990 the Plain
English Campaign has promoted the use of clear
English by awarding its Crystal Mark.

MAKE SURE ALL YOUR
DUCKS ARE IN A ROW

Workplace jargon is characterised by the application of new meanings to well-known
words. How are these words currently used in an office – cascade, ghosting, matador?

Genre

When we encounter the words 'Once upon a time', or 'Dear Madam' we have a good idea of what is coming, as these are markers of genre. Genres are largely recognisable through having distinct forms of grammar, text lengths, vocabulary or layouts.

Some of the manipulation of language that we recognise as the markers of poetry evolved very early as part of an oral culture. Alliteration, rhythm and rhyme all helped the reciter learn the text, and can be found in Old and Middle English poems, though end-rhyme was never a major feature of Old English verse. In the late fourteenth century alliteration was a strong characteristic of English poetry. In *Gawain and the Green Knight*, c.1390, this ('Sithen the siege & the assault was ceased at Troy') gives a clear indication that we are looking at poetry.

The emergence of Middle English as a literary language indicates its acceptance among the educated and leisured English. The long poem *Brut* by Layamon (c.1225) is heavily influenced by contemporary French chivalric romances, but its split-line structure and the Old English letter forms look archaic compared to the song *Sumer is icumen in* of the same period. The status of English as a literary language was enhanced by Chaucer, the 'first finder of our fair language', who according to William Caxton 'enbelysshyd, ornated and made faire our Englisshe'.

In 1742 the poet Thomas Gray wrote that 'the language of the age is never the language of poetry', thus supporting the use of 'poetic diction' and the written use of words such as 'o'er', 'methinks' or 'Poesy', which survived well into the nineteenth century.

To walk in the Visions of Poesy

The Pleasant History of John Winchcomb (1597) is considered to be the first novel written in English, but the novel became established as a genre with John Bunyan's allegorical novel *Pilgrim's Progress* (1678), Aphra Behn's *Oroonoko* (1688), and Daniel Defoe's *Robinson Crusoe* (1719). It developed as the dominant literary form through the major novels of the nineteenth century, becoming, through writers as diverse as James Joyce, Chinua Achebe and R K Narayan, a medium that celebrated both the multiculturalism of the language and the cultures that fed into it.

In the prologues and prefaces to his books, William Caxton introduced the idea of advertising into the first material printed in England in the fifteenth century, but we would more easily recognise as advertisements the promotional leaflets for cocoa printed in the 1890s. The most important quality of the cocoa here is its purity; later advertisements concentrated on other ideas – the effects of the product, real or imaginary, in terms of lifestyle changes.

A similarly persuasive use of language is found in journalism, as reportage, analysis and headline. The broadsides of the eighteenth century, announcing or recounting executions, foreshadow the tabloid newspaper, while an early newspaper, the *Oxford Gazette* of 1665, carried authoritative information about the Court.

In letters we find writing coming closest to speech. Written in the fifteenth century, the Paston letters tell of the stresses of life during the Wars of the Roses (1455–85), in conversational terms such as; the King 'is in a place in Yorkshire called Corcumbre; that is its name, or something like it'.

Twitter allows 140 characters per tweet. SMS allows 150 characters. In 1942 a Post Office telegram cost 6d for nine words, plus a penny for each extra word.

Standards

Now if any ask me, whence is it that our conversation is so much refin'd? I must freely, and without flattery, ascribe it to the Court: and, in it, particularly to the King; whose example gives a law to it.

This statement from the dramatist John Dryden in 1672 shows that standards in spoken English derived at that time not from a set of rules, but from a social structure. Eight hundred years earlier the West Saxon dialect (of the court of King Alfred) had become the standard for Old English literature, but in the Middle English period the dialect of the East Midlands and London became dominant.

> I. N. take thee. N. to my wedded wife, to haue and to hold from this day forward, for better, for wurſe, for richer, for poorer, in ſyckeneſſe, and in health, to loue, and to cheriſhe, till death vs depart: accordyng to Gods holy ordeinaunce: And therto I plight thee my trouth.

Another standard for English has been the language of the Church, particularly in the form of the *Book of Common Prayer* (1549), and various translations of the Bible, culminating in the Authorised Version (1611). Legal English, which emerged around 1350, has also provided a model for precision and clarity. During the reign of Henry V from 1413 to 1422, the king issued texts in English for judicial and governmental purposes; this 'Chancery English' was disseminated round the country, helping to circulate standards of spelling and grammar for the written language.

Books on self-improvement give an indication of standards to be aspired to; for example, *How to Talk Correctly* (1877) advised its readers to pronounce 'poignant' as 'poinant', which was maintained in Murray's *New English Dictionary* in 1909.

> **Poignant** (poi·nănt), *a.* Forms: 4-6 poynaunt, 4-8 -ant, 7-8 poinant, 7- poignant, (5 pugnaunt, ponȝeand, -yaunt, -yawnt, poygnaunt, poyngnant). [ME. a. OF. *puignant* (12th c. in Godef.), *poignant* (13th c.), pr. pple. of *poindre* :—L. *pungĕre* to prick, pierce.]

PUNCTUATION *.

PUNCTUATION is the art of dividing a written composition into sentences, or parts of sentences, by points or stops, for the purpose of marking the different pauses which the sense, and an accurate pronunciation require.

The comma represents the shortest pause ; the Semicolon, a pause double that of the comma ; the Colon, double that of the semicolon ; and the Period, double that of the colon.

Early use of punctuation in English was inconsistent, with several signs in use which have now disappeared entirely. The current system emerged during the sixteenth century, though certain forms appeared much later – the apostrophe to show possession (Pat's book) developed during the eighteenth century. The use of a capital letter at the beginning of important nouns, as recommended by John Hart in 1569, increased during the seventeenth century, but gradually decreased during the eighteenth century, though Murray's *Grammar* was still using this in describing the 'Colon' and 'Semicolon' in 1834.

There was an increase in the variety of spellings in English following the arrival of French scribes after 1066, as they struggled to spell words from speech in a range of regional accents. Variant spellings did not generally seem to cause people problems in the sixteenth century – the *Book of Common Prayer* spelled 'matins' in four different ways, and print compositors often doubled consonants and added 'e' at the ends of words to fill space in a line. Hart reacted to this confusion by offering a system in which spelling reflected contemporary pronunciation: double consonants were to be dropped, and marks adopted to show the pronunciation of vowels. Richard Mulcaster's *Elementarie* (1582) standardised the silent 'e' after a consonant to lengthen the preceding vowel – as in 'made', 'coke' or 'fine'.

Caxton, working at the end of the fifteenth century, was very aware that print involved the selection of one dialect word over another, a choice which would bring both potential confusion and standardisation, as seen in his story of the Yorkshireman who asked a Kentish woman for some eggs – she thought he was speaking French. Fortunately someone was at hand to explain that the Kentish word for 'eggs' was 'eyren'. Caxton, whose choices in these situations would go far towards setting the standard, asks the reader, 'what should a man write, "eggs" or "eyren"?'

These pronunciations were recommended in *Broadcast English*, 1929, by the Advisory Committee on Spoken English.

nevvew	(nephew)
fórred	(forehead)
cúmbat	(combat)
dékkad	(decade)
eev'l	(evil)

Accent and Dialect – The World

Some distinctive accents were noticed in America from the early seventeenth century, but American English achieved a formal difference after Independence (1776). Noah Webster's essays and dictionaries, published between 1789 and 1828, proposed different spellings as a deliberate promotion of American identity, moving on from archaic forms, particularly the use of 'k' in words like 'musick', which could still be found in Johnson's *Dictionary* in 1790. Webster removed a lot of 'unnecessary' letters, as in 'color', and rationalised other spellings such as 'theater', but some of his suggestions, such as 'tung', never stuck.

> TŎNGUE, (tung,) [Sax. *tung, tunga*; Goth. *tuggo*; Sw. *tunga*; Dan. *tunge*; D. *tong*; G. *zunge*; Ir. and Gaelic, *teanga*; Ant. L. *tingua*. We see by the Gothic, that *n* is not radical; the word belongs to Class Dg. It signifies a shoot or extension, like L. *digitus* and *dug*. Tung would be the preferable orthography, in accordance with the etymology.]

Despite this apparently progressive approach to language, American English has retained some usages which British usage has abandoned – for example 'dove' (for 'dived') and 'candy'. 'Mighty pretty' is difficult to imagine without an American accent, though it can be found in the diary of Samuel Pepys in 1667.

Some differences are difficult to explain: Why is the British 'pernickety', meaning 'fussy', 'persnickety' in America?

In many parts of the world, trade involving English gave rise to a number of limited versions of English used for business purposes, which became known as pidgins. These developed in areas such as China, the Pacific, the West Coast of North America, the Caribbean and West Africa. As the use of these developed from merely contact-languages, and as their own structures and vocabularies evolved, such languages became mother-tongues, known as creoles.

Webster's dictionaries set a model for other glossaries of English as the language developed around the world: Morris's *Austral English* (1898), the word collections of Charles Leland in the US (1850s), and the comprehensive *Hobson-Jobson* (1886). The latter, a study of Anglo-Indian English, was a wide-ranging dictionary which showed the ways that the sounds of English could be adapted to the sounds of a variety of South Asian languages, and reflected in English spelling. In some cases the results might be misleading – in India 'champagne' became 'simkin'. Many words from Indian languages were also adopted into English.

> **Pyjammas**, s. Hind. *pāĕ-jāma*, lit. 'leg-clothing.' A pair of loose drawers or trowsers, tied round the waist. Such a garment is used by various persons in India, *e.g.* by women of various classes, by Sikh men, and by most Mahommedans of both sexes. It was adopted from the Mahommedans by Europeans as an article of *dishabille* and of night attire, and is synonymous with **long-drawers** (q.v., also **Shulwaur** and **Mogul-breeches**). It is probable that we English took the habit like a good many others from the Portuguese. Thus Pyrard (c. 1610) says, in speaking of Goa Hospital : " Ils ont force *calsons* sans quoy ne couchent iamais les Portugais des Indes" (ii., p. 11). The word is now used in London shops.

Babu English grew from the need for an ornate and polite style of English to match the indigenous language patterns used in South Asia. The elaboration and use of archaisms satisfied the need in social

> " So my request to you that your sympathy and philanthropic zeal will take some measure in my part, by provide me a post either by you, or by your direct patronage, to look with a favourable eye towards me by showing some mercy and thankfulness.

and political situations for indirectness and formality.

The development after 1880 of African literature allowed the international recognition of a variety of distinctive African dialects. The second half of the twentieth century also brought greater awareness of the range of Caribbean accents and dialects through the spread of calypso and reggae, and later through the literary use of Jamaican patois in the UK by writers such as Linton Kwesi Johnson and Valerie Bloom.

Some international varieties of common words

UK	US	South Africa	New Zealand	Canada
biscuit	cookie	biscuit	biscuit	cookie
lolly	popsicle	sucker	ice block	lollipop
dummy	pacifier	dummy	dummy	soother
pavement	sidewalk	pavement	footpath	sidewalk
traffic lights	stop lights	robots	traffic lights	stop lights
chips	fries	slap chips	hot chips	chips/fries

English at Play

> A moth ate words.
> To me that seemed
> a wonderful fate
> when I heard about this wonder
> That a worm swallowed
> some words of a man
> a thief in the dark –
> a wonderful saying
> strong in its foundation.
> That thieving guest
> was none the wiser
> for having swallowed the words

The vast number of English words is just one factor that allows so many possibilities for play in the language. The Anglo-Saxons enjoyed riddles, Middle English writers played on the ambiguities caused by punctuation, and the Elizabethan and Stuart wits used extended metaphors and allegories to simultaneously hide and reveal meaning. Puns can be found at most periods of English, and Caxton's successor printed a book of jokes. Finding successfully playful use of English, such as 'drinka pinta milka day' from the 1970s, is the goal of the highest-paid advertising copy-writers, and millions are delighted by slips of the tongue or typewriter – blunders like those reported in Colemanballs in *Private Eye*.

Shakespeare's wordplay in Sonnets 135 and 136 (1609) encompass practically all the possible contemporary meanings of the word 'will', to do with time, desire, intention, sex and the poet's name. This kind of dexterity was not just to do with smart young men displaying their cleverness: 20 years later John Donne as Dean of St Pauls applied the same technique in *Hymn to God the Father*, one of his Holy Sonnets: 'When thou hast done, thou hast not done'.

The Anglo-Saxon enjoyment of words is seen in the frequent use in verse of 'kennings', metaphors whose meaning is clear to those in the know; thus 'sea' becomes 'whale-path', and 'swords', in the tenth-century poem *Battle of Brunanburh*, becomes the 'leavings of hammers'. The same principle is at work in *The Masquerade* (1800) with the anagrams, riddles and charades transposed from the mead-hall to the parlour.

The spelling of text messages may raise the hackles of purists, but this kind of playful and deliberately disruptive approach to spelling has a long history. Bombaugh's *Gleanings from the Harvest-fields of Literature* (1867) includes phrases such as 'I wrote 2 U B 4', which might have been lifted directly from a mobile phone.

Charles Lutwidge Dodgson played with his own first two names to give the pseudonym Lewis Carroll, under which he wrote the *Alice* books, which are full of wordplay, satire and verbal wit. The poetry of Edward Lear, which established the idea of nonsense as a literary form, is closer to children's rhymes, often maintaining their sense of melancholy and darkness.

ESSAY TO MISS CATHARINE JAY.

An S A now I mean 2 write
  2 U sweet K T J,
The girl without a ‖,
  The belle of U T K.

I 1 der if U got that I
  I wrote 2 U B 4
I sailed in the R K D A,
  And sent by L N Moore.

My M T head will scarce contain
  A calm I D A bright
But A T miles from U I must
  M—- this chance 2 write.

And 1st, should N E N V U,
  B E Z, mind it not,
Should N E friendship show, B **true**:
  They should not B forgot.

From virt U nev R D V 8;
  Her influence B 9
A like induces 10 dern S,
  Or 40 tude D vine.

The contents of *A Hundred Mery Talys* (1526) the first known book of jokes originating in English, mostly tend more towards moral fables than side-splitting one-liners, but show national stereotypes as the butt for jokes. Joke-books recur through the history of printing in English, with three new titles being published every two days in 2010.

Maybe 'play' consists of breaking the rules. Robert Graves said 'a poet has to master the rules of grammar before he attempts to bend or break them', and much of English literature does indeed consist of bending or breaking perceived rules. The works of James Joyce and e e cummings show authors playing with forms and words, teasing the reader's expectations and assumptions, and using word-choice, punctuation and spacing to reinvigorate the relationship between writer and reader.

Manypeeplia Upsidownia

The longest palindrome (a word reading the same forwards and backwards) in the *Oxford English Dictionary* is 'tattarrattat'. Invented by James Joyce in *Ulysses* (1922) it means 'a knock on the door'.

Rules and Fashions

It seems we have never been able to avoid correcting other people's English. In the Worcester version of the *Anglo-Saxon Chronicle* a scribe altered an earlier writer's spelling of 'Lindisfarne'. Around 1200 the scribe Orrm attempted to create a spelling system that gave phonetic direction, by standardising the doubling of consonants to indicate the pronunciation of a preceding short vowel – as in 'crisstenndom'. As the main reason for his reorganisation of spelling and use of marks to show vowel length was to show other readers how to read texts aloud, this process can be considered as one of 'making rules'.

Rules often derive from rationalisation and attempts to bring order to what was perceived by Jonathan Swift in 1712 as a language which 'in many instances ... offended against every part of Grammar'. But just as attempts to fix English have always been rejected, so rules change, as language changes. The 1973 edition of Fowler's *The King's English* noted that 'different to' was 'gaining ground, and will probably displace "different from" in no long time.' This is less to do with rationalisation than with fashion; 'different than' must now be added to the mix.

In the eighteenth century grammarians enthusiastically laid down the rules for 'correct' English as the descriptive process became applied as prescriptive. But much of this depended on trying to shoehorn English into a Latin pattern, with case endings, tenses and even noun genders, according to long-standing ideas of the supremacy of Latin and Greek.

specious Name of *Anglicisme*. And have no other way to clear my doubts, but by translating my English into Latine, and thereby trying what sence the words will bear in a more stable language. I am desirous if it were possible, that we might all write with the same certainty of words and purity of phrase, to which the Italians first arriv'd, and after them the French: At least

This process occasionally produced absurdities, as when Murray suggested in 1843 that the existence of the gender-specific ending –ess , as in 'actress' implied that 'when we say of a woman, she is a philosopher, an astronomer, a builder, a weaver, we perceive an impropriety in the termination, which we cannot avoid'.

Changes in the language frustrated expectations of the absoluteness of rules. Henry Alford, in the second edition of his *Plea for the Queen's English* (1864), acknowledged that he had received complaints and challenges, and was aware that his guidelines would outrage many readers. Then as now, difficulties over the use of the apostrophe indicate that standards could be interpreted in different ways.

> THE fact, that an edition consisting of an unusually large number of copies of this little work has been exhausted in a few months, shews that the Public are not indifferent to the interest of the subject. The course of the controversy which it has excited has at all events shewn one thing : that its publication was not un-needed. And though, in the course of this controversy, I have received some hard hits, I have no reason to complain, seeing that it has continually furnished me, as it has gone on, with fresh material for new remarks, and ampler justification for those which I had already made.

The debate over rules continued into the twentieth century in publications such as Fowler's *Modern English Usage* and Strunk & White's *The Elements of Style* in the US. When grammar is taught in British schools today, it is sometimes based on memories of 'rules' from these texts, passed down through up to four generations.

i before e except after c
i before e except after c
i before e except after c
i before e except after c
i before e except after c
i before e except after c
i before e except after c
i before e except after c
i before e except after c

In *Politics and the English Language* (1946), George Orwell proposed six rules for writing good English. The last of them was: 'Break any of these rules sooner than say anything outright barbarous.'

One of Us – Inclusion and Exclusion

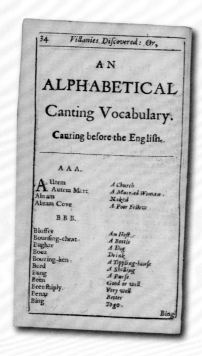

The use of language to keep outsiders out and limit intelligible communication to insiders ranges from the jargon of medieval alchemists ('jargon' originally meaning 'gibberish') to the constantly changing vocabulary of Multicultural London English. For centuries marginalised or disenfranchised groups have manipulated English in ways that act as markers of group identity.

Among the clearest uses of exclusion in English is cockney rhyming slang. Now thought to be dying out in its traditional heartland, it occasionally appears as a geographical marker in *Eastenders*, but perhaps its demise was begun when it became a quaint theatrical device (as in Shaw's *Pygmalion*) rather than a system for criminals to hide their intentions from snooping police officers. Slang has served this purpose for centuries – Richard Head's 1673 *Canting Academy* was written to help the public protect themselves by being able to recognise criminal slang. Similar works were published as early as 1552.

A few cockney rhyming slang phrases have generally lost their rhyming markers and become well-used terms (e.g. 'to blow a raspberry' from 'raspberry tart'). But the inventiveness survives: 1980s City traders used to lend each other a 'Pavarotti' (£10, a 'tenner'), reinforcing the spoken rather than written nature of the slang.

Such forms of exclusive language are not limited to criminals: in fact nineteenth century London police used the word 'starling' for a person seen committing an offence – the culprit was, like the starling, 'spotted'.

Blab—a prating stupid fellow, a fool	Blow —to split, tell, expose	Bolt—cut, go, make yourself scarce	Boxed—locked up
Blab, to—to nose, to chatter, to tell secrets	Blow me tight—a sort of burlesque oath; as, If I don't I'm jigger'd, &c.	Bolted—hopped the twig, shuffled, gone	Boxing a Charley—upsetting a watchman in his box
Black beetles—the lower order of people	Blowings—prostitutes	Bone – to steal	Brads—money
Black diamonds—coals, or coalheavers	Blue ruin—gin	Bone box—the mouth	Brass—impudence
Black boy—a clergyman	Blue devils, blues—low spirits, horror struck	Bone setter—a hackney coach	Bracket face – devilish ugly
Black Indies—castle	Blue pigeon filers, or flyers —thieves who steal lead from the tops of houses and churches	Bonnetter —a thump on the hat	Bravoes—bullies
Black-... vine		Bon vivant—a choice spirit, a jolly dog	Bread basket – the stomach
Black ...—a lawyer		Booth—a place for harbouring thieves	Breaking shins–- borrowing money
Black s... mer		Booked—in for it, dished	Breeze, kicking up a—exciting a disturbance
Black ... picking	Blubber—to whine, to cry	Booze—drink	Brisket-beater—a Roman Catholic
Black locks	Bl... to bluster, look big	Boozy—drunk	Brick—a loaf
Black ...—a ...ler or tu...	B...—an...pudent im...g fe...w of an inn-	Boozing ken—a lush crib, a sluicery, ale-house	Broads—cards
Black-le... ...ers, fellows who la... and after losing ...y them ; a prof...bler	...a stupid igno-... fellow ...ip, rag. money g sch...—a house of ...ction. ...prison	Bore—a tedious story, or a vexatious circumstance	Brogue—Irish accent
		Bordell—a bawdyken, house of ill fame	Broom—go, cut, be gone
		Bottle-head—stupid, void of sense	Browns—copper coin
Black hou... ...sons		Bought — any thing that's dearly paid for	Brown Bess—a soldier's firelock
...fr... ...ey— ...ttery, ...mon ...ers—...sh...p ...s—...he...stee...er	B...stick—a... Be...il—a l... ...stitute...	Bounce—to lie, to swagger	Brown suit—no go
	...'s assistant ..., a shilling ...woman, or		Brown gater droppings, heavy wet, heavy brown, beer
			Brush, or buy a brush—be off make yourself scarce
			Brusher—a full glass

In the nineteenth century slang and cant dictionaries, such as those by Andrewes and Kent, both forewarned and entertained those not in the know, with their listings of words used by the criminal underclass, the sporting fraternity and fashionable young men.

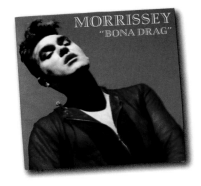

Polari, twentieth century gay slang, came to public ears through a BBC Radio comedy in the 1960s. It is difficult to know whether words such as 'camp', 'naff', 'glossies', 'bona' or 'dish' were adopted by or came out of Polari, but these are certainly no longer exclusive to the gay community.

When the psychologist Eugene Landy was compiling
The Underground Dictionary in 1971 he asked what the word 'groovy' meant; he was told:

'Groovy means groovy, man'.

This kind of invented word deliberately defies translation, as part of creating an alternative way of knowing the world.

Some now common words started out as student slang, such as posh, mob, toff, and bus.

Today, a student would want to avoid graduationg with a Desmond (Tutu), although a Thora Hird would be even less desirable.

Education

The majority of surviving Old English manuscripts originated in the tenth century and are the legacy of the programme of literary restoration set in place by Alfred the Great in an attempt to repair some of the cultural havoc caused by the Viking invasions. Many of these texts were translations from Latin, but they include the *Anglo-Saxon Chronicle*, a record of notable events, maintained until the middle of the twelfth century.

Several glossaries and translations for educational purposes were made during the Old English period. *The Vespasian Psalter* was the first part of the Bible to be translated, in the ninth century, followed by the *Lindisfarne Gospels* in the tenth century; these translations were for clerics who were not proficient in Latin.

By 1387 people were already learning foreign languages on the grounds of their value when travelling. *Here is a good boke to lerne to speke French* (1496) gives an idea of what it was like for a French-speaker to learn English.

By the end of the fourteenth century English was in a secure position as the language of education: when John of Trevisa translated Higden's *Polychronicon*, he was able to say that 'children leveth Frensch' to do their learning in 'englysch'. The emphasis at this time was to learn 'grammar', though later 'grammar schools' were founded specifically for the teaching of Latin rather than English grammar.

During the sixteenth century, literacy levels rose as the Reformation led to the Bible and prayerbooks being read in English; by 1600 there were half a million Bibles for a population of six million. A hornbook (a handheld frame containing printed text) from this period shows the text of the Lord's Prayer, indicating the link between reading and faith.

Hornbooks were often attached to a child's clothes, as if to fix the learning physically. In the seventeenth century the structure of teaching was based on teaching children to read from the age of seven and to write from the age of eight; but as eight was also the recognised age for starting work, many children learned to read but not write.

In the nineteenth century many children left school for an apprenticeship having completed a copy-book, effectively an account of all they had learned, and proof that they could write. But not all education was rote-learning: books such as *The Infant's Grammar* and *The Good Child's Book of Stops*, from the mid-1820s, introduced novelty and colour into the learning of grammar and punctuation.

Textbooks in specialist areas pre-date the introduction of printing, and were to become a stable source of income for publishers. John Smith's manual for new sailors *An Accidence for Young Sea-men* (1626) stayed in print for 65 years. Wynkyn de Worde's *Proprytees & Medicynes of Hors* (1497–8) is the earliest known English book on veterinary medicine, and the printed book has proved the ideal means of providing instruction and reference for any trade or vocation. In 1996, according to Unesco Institute for Statistics, works in the social and applied sciences made up 45% of all book titles published in the UK.

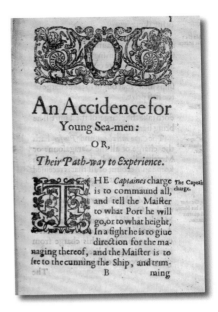

THE PRONOUNS

Many primary schools use spelling tests as a way of teaching children spelling. Should they teach grammar in the same way?

Swe@r!ng

Printing the word 'bugger' was a criminal offence until 1929 (according to Eric Partridge's *Dictionary of Slang and Unconventional English*, 1937, it once meant 'a stealer of breastpins from fellow drunks') but is now a fairly mild expletive. On the other hand, the F-word was in the seventeenth century part of a common word for a kestrel (f***wind), and can be found in Chapman's translation of Homer (1616).

THE WATER IS RIGHT UP TO MY EXPECTATIONS

One function fulfilled by swearing is to provide us with a ready-made set of powerful words for moments when the language part of our brains may not work at its best. Few of us when in the middle of a heated argument would be able to come up with such an ingenious insult as Dr Johnson's 'Sir, your wife under pretence of being a bawdy-house keeper, is a receiver of stolen goods.'

But at the same time swearing is a field in which language is developed most inventively, particularly in creating its own levels of acceptability, by which 'Christ' could be toned down to 'crikey', 'cripes', and 'crums', and in such constructions as 'abso-bloody-lutely'.

A few taboo words describing body parts started out as the 'normal' forms in Old English; one of the markers of the status difference between Anglo-Norman and Old English is the way the 'English' version became unacceptable, while the 'French' version became the polite or scientific term. The Old English 'scitte' gave way to the Anglo-Norman 'ordure' and later the Latin-via-French 'excrement'.

The British media currently maintains fairly recognisable positions on how taboo words are used, ranging from the *Guardian*'s use of the F-word, to a watershed, after which a range of words can be used on television. If all the words that are currently taboo become acceptable, will we have to invent new swear words to shock ourselves with?

Eric Partridge described his working process while researching for *A Dictionary of Slang and Unconventional English*: 'I read widely, moved in many circles, and listened hard; necessarily, I listened very discreetly, wherever I might be prosecuting my researches.'

ARSE. ſ. [earre, Sax.] The buttocks. To hang an ARSE : To be tardy, ſluggiſh.

Some words have gradually become acceptable over the past few decades, though we might not know that they had been fully acceptable terms long ago. For example, 'arse' appears in many eighteenth century dictionaries.

Many online multiplay game websites are stringent about the use of swearing; users have reacted by creating new words, such as 'noob', which convey meanings of abuse without being caught by swearing-recognition programs.

ods bodkins. A joc. exclam, a late C.19–20 perversion of *ods bodikins*, lit. God's little bodies, a C.17–19 oath. See **ods.**

Supposedly William I tried to learn English but only learned to swear – and we still use the term 'Anglo-Saxon' to describe certain taboo words. Some insults in use today have earlier origins than you might imagine, for example 'bum' (Middle English, but not considered rude until the late eighteenth century) and 'arse' (at least 1000 years old). 'Nutcase' is from the 1960s and so is 'plonker', though the latter became more popular in the 1980s.

Change – Now

The use of English as the main language of the internet has accelerated both the spread of the language throughout the world and its development, especially among non-native speakers. Within the British Isles English continues to be influenced by speech-patterns from elsewhere.

There is considerable dispute about the influence of television on accent and dialect; what is clear is that distinctions between groups of speakers remain, and there is little prospect of the majority of the population speaking Estuary English, any more than West Coast American Valley or Uptalk (speech intonation with a rising pitch). Television does have an impact on vocabulary, but changes in patterns of pronunciation depend more on direct contact.

'Ax' for 'ask' was used in the UK in many areas well into the twentieth century, but died out, to be returned via the Caribbean, echoing the way that some Celtic words came back to Britain through French adoption of Breton words (e.g. 'car' and 'gravel'). Similarly, some older or regional British English usages are now returning from America: for example, 'mall', once a sheltered walk, now a pedestrian shopping area, or 'cookie', once Scottish but becoming more widespread after re-importation.

There is a perceived increase in the use of American English, though it may be that this derives in large part from the success of some chains of American restaurants and shops using terms such as 'coffee to go', or 'regular' rather than 'standard'. A quick internet search for 'muffin' reveals first a 'muffin' (an American soft cake) and then an 'English muffin'.

Regular
super-skinny
chocca-mocha
latte with an
extra shot
(no foam)
to go

Perhaps the clearest change happening now is the blurring of once clearly recognised registers. Some youth-speak terms have entered mainstream usage, so that many adults would feel at ease with saying they had been 'disrespected' by someone with 'issues' or too much 'attitude'. During the 2010 General Election a prime-ministerial candidate told another to 'get real': he had probably been told to speak with the 'common touch', using words from a lower register than would normally be used in a governmental context.

If changes in language usage reflect changes in the way a society thinks, what are we to make of the way that 'respect' is now such a widely used term, and an 'act of God' is primarily an insurance assessor's get-out clause? Formerly widely understood terms of reference such as 'honour', 'modesty', 'virtue' and 'valour' have lost much of their meaning, reflecting the abandonment of widely accepted, if conservative, morals. We are now more likely to use terms borrowed from the sciences – 'mania', 'post-traumatic stress disorder', 'tsunami' and 'global warming' – as we are exposed to more diverse kinds of information.

How many different forms do you use to greet someone? Hi, hello, hiya, how do you do, hey, 'allo, good morning? When do you use them? Do you ever use the wrong one?

get real
alright?
greetings
wotcha

good afternoon

'ow do?
how ya doin'

hi hello hiya how do you do? yo
hey wassssup? g'day now then
morning good morning
howdy 'allo good evening ay up

An acronym is a word made from the initial letters of a phrase, for example ASBO (Anti-Social Behaviour Order). The word 'podcast' looks like an acronym, but initially wasn't. A 'backronym' was invented to explain it: Personal On Demand broadcast.

Getting it Wrong

For a language that is used by so many people, English seems to have a remarkable number of problems and inconsistencies that we tend to ignore.

Why is it that Standard English uses 'defunct' but not 'to defunction', 'to malfunction' but not 'malfunct', 'functional' and 'dysfunctional' but not 'defunctional' or 'malfunctional'? Given that English has developed in a way that echoes Darwinian evolution, by chance mutations, some inconsistencies look almost deliberately absurd.

In June 2010 the *Appropriate Language Guide* produced for the Lothian and Borders Police advised police to stop using the terms 'love', 'pet' and 'dear' when addressing women, while in 2005 a woman who was hit by a car was told off by a police officer for describing the driver as 'fat'. Yet expressions of outrage at **PC LANGUAGE GONE MAD!** sound reactionary and unwilling to face the reality that the use of language expresses social power structures.

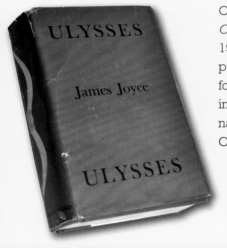

Obscenity legislation prevented D H Lawrence's *Lady Chatterley's Lover* from being published in Britain until 1960, 32 years after its initial publication in Florence. The publication of James Joyce's *Ulysses* was similarly hindered for decades in Britain and the US. Regulations governing indecency and profanity, administered by the curiously named Master of the Revels from 1574, would have banned Chaucer from the late-Elizabethan stage.

Until the middle of the twentieth century schoolchildren were urged to avoid the use of 'nice' and 'get', and for many there remains the shadow of disapproval for sentences ending with a preposition. So, rather than saying 'these are words we feel we ought to avoid ending a sentence with', we should say 'these are words with which we ought to avoid ending a sentence'. Of course it doesn't work, and famously provoked Churchill's comment, 'this is the sort of English up with which I will not put.'

The dialect word 'innit' (for example 'I'm going home, innit') has its origins in spoken rather than written English. When spoken, the final sound is a glottal stop (a catch in the throat that is a spoken alternative to 't'). However, when written it ends with a 't'. Is this use of a 't' to denote the glottal stop a nod in the direction of 'correct' spelling and pronunciation – and surprising given the informal origins of the word?

Spelling reform revived in the nineteenth century alongside Isaac Pitman's shorthand system; less tortuous were the reforms proposed by the Simplifyd Speling Sosiëty of the 1920s. Pitman's attempts to reform spelling influenced the Initial Teaching Alphabet, which was used in some British schools in 1961, with titles such as *Goeing Too Scool*. These were intended to help children to learn to spell.

> Gerlz and boiz
>   Kum out tu plai,
> Dhe moon duz shyn
>   Az bryt az dai;
> Leev eur super
>   And leev eur sleep,
> Kum tu eur plai-feloez
>   In dhe street.
>
> Kum widh a whoop
>   And kum widh a kaul,
> Kum widh a good-wil
>   Or not at aul;
> Up dhe lader
>   And doun dhe waul,
> A peni loef
>   Wil serv eu aul.

It was noted in the mid-eighteenth century that avocado or avigato pears were being called 'alligator pears'. In the seventeenth century asparagus developed into 'sparagrass' and then 'sparrowgrass'. The Spanish 'castaña' became the English 'chestnut', despite having no connection with chests or nuts.

'Ortgeard' became 'orceard' and then 'orchard' as spelling followed pronunciation. What other words are ripe for this kind of rationalisation? Should Tuesday become Chewsday?

Power and Class

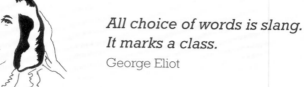

All choice of words is slang.
It marks a class.
George Eliot

The word 'runes' means 'secret' or 'hidden', reminding us of the basic link between literacy, language and power. Words still hold power over us: we use euphemisms to avoid direct utterances to do with major adverse events such as military action or death. Old English even avoided directly saying 'die' altogether.

To a certain extent class distinctions in English derive from the trilingual nature of post-Conquest England, which created a pattern of different areas of activity being carried out by speakers from different backgrounds. Historically power has been the key to this. For example, the name of the Battle of Hastings tells us who the victors were: if Harold had been victorious we would probably know it as the Fight of Hastings (the eleventh-century poem called *The Battle of Maldon* uses the Old English word 'gefeoht'). Thus a 'battle' is more formal and serious than a 'fight'.

In the thirteenth and fourteenth centuries there was a second wave of adoption of words from France, from the fashionable French of Paris. By 1350 French and English were in competition, but the clearest marker of the prevalence of English can be seen in its being used for the opening of Parliament in 1362.

Chaucer's choice of words shows the social status of the people he describes. In the Prologue to the *Canterbury Tales* the Miller, an earthy character, is described mostly in monosyllabic Norse- and Old English-based words, such as 'byg' and 'broad', while for the Prioress, who aspires to something finer, Chaucer increases his use of words adopted from French, such as 'plesaunt' and 'amiable'.

But it is a difgrace to a gentleman, to be guilty of falfe fpelling, either by omitting, changing, or adding letters contrary to cuf-tom; and yet it fhall be no difgrace to omit letters, or even fyllables in fpeaking, and to huddle his words fo together, as to render them utterly unintelligible.

By the mid-eighteenth century competence in spelling was viewed as a necessary social accomplishment, as seen in Sheridan's 1762 *Lectures on Elocution*.

Certain words have acted as social markers – 'bloody' was particularly associated with the lower class in the early twentieth century, while the upper class gradually abandoned 'ain't' after it became associated in the nineteenth century with the lower classes. But since the eighteenth century there has been fashionable upper-class adoption of lower-class language, which happened frequently where classes mixed, as at boxing matches – 'ivories' for 'teeth' for example. Nancy Mitford in *Noblesse Oblige* (1956) played on the way language defined and was defined by class, but sometimes apparently switched polarities. Thus 'pudding' and 'what?' were 'U' (upper class), while 'sweet' and 'pardon?' were 'non-U'.

'Midwifery' is a word which derives from Old English rather than Latin or Greek, implying that historically it has been given a lower status than other branches of medicine. It is no coincidence that it has been predominantly practised by women.

Poor teenagers – while mangling of the language by adults gets to be an accent or a dialect, it is the young who get the blame for lazy grammar, spelling that dumps centuries of gradual change, and bizarre shifts in the uses of words that makes a good thing 'wicked' and an attractive person both 'hot' and 'cool'. Attempts by adults to adopt the same usages are ridiculed, as in the BBC programming for 'Yoof' in the 1990s.

Yet teenagers are traditionally the most inventive users of English, creating such words as 'skeen', 'hench', and 'cotching'. Perhaps a position of challenge to authority allows the ease of movement across fields of use – so that 'Oh My God' can transfer to the text-form 'omg' and then back to speech as 'O-M-G'; or the text-form 'lol' (laugh out loud) becomes a spoken word expressing amused approval.

Differences and changes tend to stand out more than continuity, but teenagers in fact mostly maintain local accents, despite the anxiety that Estuary is creeping out from the South East like some invasive plant. And a lot of teenage usage is very localised. Despite the internet and the popularity of websites such as Urban Dictionary, situations arise where 'skeen' may be used in Croydon, but unknown in East Grinstead, 20 miles away. Localised use of Facebook may reinforce local usages – for example, boosting the use of 'nerks' for 'chips' in Leeds and Huddersfield.

The blurred ethnicity of youth in many large urban centres has provided an ideal forum for the adoption of speech patterns and usages across previously separate groups. Sometimes this is deliberately imitative, as in Ali G-type speech, sometimes less so. The use of phrases such as 'I am so going to miss this train' is fairly clearly derived from US West Coast Valley Speak, while the idea that rising intonation at the end of a phrase derives from Australian or American TV is widely disputed. The exclusivity of 'youth-speak' can be seen when older generations try to use it: attempts to 'translate' the Bible or Shakespeare or Dickens into modern youth-speak are seen by some as patronising, and merely by virtue of being published they miss the point of an oral verbal culture.

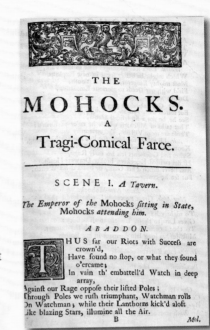

One particularly noted phenomenon is the spoken use of 'I was like ...' or 'I turned round and ...' in place of 'I said ...'. These apparently rootless changes annoy many, yet they seem to contradict accusations of laziness (both are longer than 'I said ...'). Incidentally they confirm the arbitrary nature of the link between what is meant and the sounds that convey it.

There is a respectable antiquity to the way that young people have borrowed terms from America: in early-eighteenth century London a gang of young aristocrats called themselves 'Mohocks'.

Vincentio, de Duke of de Vienna turf, decided to take time off from being de Duke and chill, so he made his main man Angelo his deputy to rule in his place, which Angelo fought was well wicked.

from *To Be Or Not To Be Innit* (2008) by Martin Baum.

500 Years of Argument

Shakespeare is credited with an extraordinary capacity to push English to its limits, and over 1800 words are attributed to Shakespeare in the *Oxford English Dictionary*. What links the following word inventions is Shakespeare's ability to turn existing parts into meaningful compounds: 'go-between', 'countless', 'laughable', 'well-read'. 'Hint', 'castigate', and 'tranquil' are just three words whose first documented use is by Shakespeare, but what happened to his 'irregulous' and 'dispunge'?

> *Enob.* Oh Soveraigne Miſtris of true Melancholly,
> The poyſonous dampe of night diſpunge upon me,
> That life, a very Rebell to my will,
> May hang no longer on me. Throw my heart
> Againſt the flint and hardneſſe of my fault,

What constitutes an acceptable invention? Is it a case of 'when I use a word, it means just what I choose it to mean, neither more nor less' as Humpty Dumpty says in *Through the Looking-Glass*? Can anyone just invent a word?

T S Eliot felt 'television' was 'ugly because of foreignness or ill-breeding', because its constituent parts come from Greek and Latin. Few now would worry about 'television', but the use of foreign words to create new English ones was a major cause for debate in Renaissance Britain. Purists complained that bringing in foreign words, known as 'inkhorn terms', would stunt the development of native words; some writers tried to revive Middle English terms such as 'algate' for 'always', or to create 'real English' words, such as 'crossed' for 'crucified'.

The revival of interest in Anglo-Saxon culture in the nineteenth century led to renewed attempts to replace Latinate words with Old English-derived forms. William Barnes proposed the use of 'folkwain' in place of 'bus'.

'Hopefully' has caused some distress; it has been suggested that since this follows a common pattern ('sadly', 'honestly', 'curiously') distaste for the usage stems from its coming from America. Yet British English has adopted other American terms such as 'OK', 'up-front', 'utility' and 'mad' (for 'angry', an older British usage).

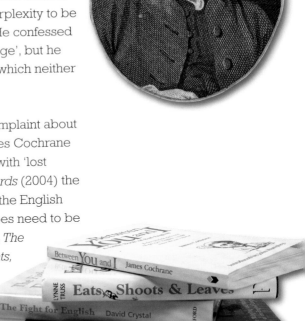

The eighteenth century saw the great debate over whether English should be 'fixed' or not. Jonathan Swift in 1712 felt 'that it is better a Language should not be perfect, than that it should be perpetually changing'. Samuel Johnson found 'our speech copious without order, and energetick without rules; wherever I turned my view, there was perplexity to be disentangled, and confusion to be regulated'. He confessed that he toyed with the idea of 'fixing our language', but he eventually feared that this was an 'expectation which neither reason nor experience can justify'.

This debate is revived every time there is a complaint about the supposed debasement of English. For James Cochrane in *Between You and I* (2003) English is littered with 'lost causes', and for John Humphrys in *Lost For Words* (2004) the problem is 'the mangling and manipulating of the English language'. 'Change can't be stopped, but it does need to be managed', was the opinion of David Crystal in *The Fight for English* (2006) while Lynne Truss's *Eats, Shoots & Leaves* (2003) highlighted 'a world of plummeting punctuation standards'. The only thing to be said for sure is that while English changes the debate will continue.

The prescriptive approach has its attractions, but few would support the implied absolutism in Lynne Truss's *Eats, Shoots and Leaves*, subtitled 'The zero tolerance approach to punctuation'. Would you put a hyphen between 'zero' and 'tolerance'?

Words In

It would be difficult to find a language which has not in some way shaped at least one word that has been adopted into the English language. While many have come from Latin via French, or from Germanic or Norse languages, others have made their way halfway round the world and back again.

The completeness of the Anglo-Saxon takeover in the fifth and sixth centuries can be seen in the number of Celtic words which were adopted into English at this time. Apart from place names there are fewer than ten which have survived into Standard English, and they are heavily disputed.

When you are tucking into an Indian takeaway on the sofa in front of the television, you are using words that have arrived via Dutch, Norse, Arabic, French, Greek and Latin. If that takeaway happens to be Vindaloo, you are using a word which travelled from Latin to Portuguese to Konkani in India and then on to English.

Different periods of history have seen words associated with particular activities being brought from specific areas. For example, during the Anglo-Saxon period the Church brought 'abbot', 'organ' and 'creed' from Latin; medieval chivalry brought 'courtesy' and 'honour' from French; the crusades brought 'saffron' and 'sugar' from the Middle East; marine engineering in the seventeenth century brought 'pump' and 'derrick' from Dutch; while science has used mainly Greek and Latin for the construction of words such as 'atmosphere' and 'equinox'.

SA'FFRON. *n. f.* [*fafran*, French, from *faphar*, Arabick. was yellow, according to *Davies* in his Welfh dictionar, *Crocus*, Latin.]

Words Out

Just as the import of various kinds of goods and ideas into Britain meant the importing of words, so the export of British goods, activities and technologies around the world has been accompanied by the export of vocabulary. Russian has adopted several English words for sporting terms, including during the nineteenth century the words 'sport' and 'sportsman' in the hunting sense. When transcribed from Cyrillic script Russian has the footballing terms 'bek', 'havbek', and 'havtajm'; other terms were more Russianised – 'boksirowat' for 'box' and 'tennisistka' for 'tennis-player'. Russian also acquired vocabulary from British railway engineering and design, including the word 'vagzal' for a station building, derived from Vauxhall Station in South London.

вокзал [vag-zāl] *sm.* railway station

English has repaid centuries of adopting words from across the Channel, by giving French 'le sandwich', 'le brainstorming', 'le cookie' and 'loguer' (to log on); French linguistic guardians have not always welcomed these. American English is probably the main current source for English terms via films, television and the internet – in 1994 French Government officials claimed their campaign to stop the adoption of English words was not anti-American. Ironically, the French term for an English person, 'un rosbif', came from two words, 'roast' and 'beef', which English had adopted from French.

In some cases, adopting a spoken English word while maintaining the host language's spelling renders it momentarily unrecognisable – Spanish has güisqui for 'whisky' and Welsh has siocled for 'chocolate'. In other cases the local adaptation of an English word has clashed with an existing word: thus Italian created 'scannare', meaning 'to scan a document', though there was already a word 'scannare', meaning 'to slaughter'.

Conclusion – Where Next?

Many people care about – and vociferously worry about – the English language. Perceived threats include an increase in the number of expressions being imported from America, the loss of potential nuances of meaning as children are no longer taught the structures of grammar, and the loss of regional accent and dialect. Mostly these are unfounded: in fact fewer words are imported from American English than from many other languages. Fiction writing seems to be in good health. And in Britain regional accents are increasingly appreciated and promoted.

Received Pronunciation has lost much of its prestige, as seen in the BBC policy of increased use of regional voices since the 1970s. The youngest generation of the Royal Family have even been heard using the glottal stop in place of 't'.

In fact there are instances of English apparently returning to its roots. Geoffrey Hughes in *Words in Time* (1988) noted the increased use of expressions made from sticking shorter words together, natural to Germanic languages, as in the phrase 'super economy double cheeseburger'; and the increased use of Latin prefixes such as 'mini-' or 'hyper-' and the use of 'plus', 'minus', 'anti' and 'pro' as independent words. The composition of phrases such as 'Sloane-ranger' or 'waste-disposal operative' approaches the playful way Old English kennings hid meanings by metaphorical word selection. But attempts to be 'Politically Correct' can take us into a world of absurdity peopled by 'static traffic managers' (parking attendants) or even 'glass clarification optimisers' (window cleaners).

Americanisms are still liable to be perceived as inappropriate arrivals, a modern equivalent of inkhorn terms. When a BBC correspondent answering a question on the Gulf oil leak in 2010 said 'guys [are] running around with their pants on fire', she felt it necessary to add – 'not literally'.